MOODS OF MANN

MOODS OF MANN

*A photographic essay
of the Isle of Man
in all its moods*

MOODS OF MANN LIMITED

MOODS OF MANN is published by Moods of Mann Limited.
Thie-ny-Chibbyr, Surby, Isle of Man, IM9 6TA.
Telephone: 01624 835656, Facsimile: 01624 836055.

Copyright © Moods of Mann Limited 1994
First published November 1994. This edition, November 1996

ISBN 0 9524304 6 0

British Library Cataloguing-in-Publication Data
A catalogue record for this book is available from the British Library.

Great care has been taken throughout this book to ensure that all details are accurate.
However, the publishers cannot accept responsibility for errors that may occur.

Joint Editors	Robin Bigland, Michael Ingram, Rick Tomlinson,
Consultant Editor	David Porteous
Contributing Writers	Terry Cringle, John Kitto,
	Margery West, Sir David Wilson
Additional written material	Michael Ingram
Additional photographic material	Rick Tomlinson
Design & Layout	Rick Tomlinson Associates / CE Marketing
Printed by	Fulmar Colour Printing Company Limited

ACKNOWLEDGMENTS

The editors would like to thank all those who have assisted in this publication.

BIBLIOGRAPHY

Statistics and details relating to the Island's financial sector have been taken from the relevant publications
with the permission of the Isle of Man Government Commercial Development Division.

Extract from 'Ballaglass Glen' by Kathleen Faragher. From 'By the Red Fuchsia Tree'. Pub. Norris Modern Press Ltd. 1967.

Extracts from 'The Collected Poems of T E Brown' Pub. Macmillan & C0. 1900.
Courtesy Manx National Heritage (previously Manx Museum and National trust) 1976.

For factual verification reference has also been made to a number of leaflets produced by the
Department of Tourism, Leisure and Transport whose assistance is gratefully acknowledged.

The Isle of Man by R H Kinvig. Liverpool University Press 1975.

Title Page Photograph: Peel Promenade in wintry sunlight.
BY ROSEMARY GREENWOOD

Contents Page Photograph: Tholt-e-Will waterfall.
BY ROSEMARY GREENWOOD

PHOTOGRAPHED BY JEREMY PAUL

PHOTOGRAPHED BY SIMON PARK

CONTENTS

PHOTOGRAPHED BY SIMON PARK

THE LIEUTENANT GOVERNOR OF THE ISLE OF MAN

His Excellency Air Marshal Sir Laurence Jones, KCB, AFC, CIMgt.

I was delighted to be asked to contribute in the production of this new publication. There have been many books, articles and poems that praise the virtues of Ellan Vannin, but no book which captures the essence and spirit of the island in photographic record. We now have a lovely addition to the record in this beautiful portrayal of island life. The book illustrates past and present and shows the long and unique heritage of stable, democratic rule enjoyed by all who live here.

Although I have lived here for only a few years, I can readily identify with the beauty and quality of life enjoyed by the populace, and it is easy to imagine this book gracing many a coffee table or library in homes around the world to remind those who know the island of its many beauties. Indeed, for those who have never visited, it provides a useful and memorable illustration of the island.

I congratulate the directors, sponsors and all who have generously supported this excellent publication. I am sure that Moods of Mann will be treasured for its portrayal of our lovely island and will appeal to all who have been captivated by its beauty.

Laurence Jones

LIEUTENANT GOVERNOR. 1994.

THE CHIEF MINISTER OF THE ISLE OF MAN GOVERNMENT
The Hon. M. R. Walker, C.B.E., M.H.K.

As Chief Minister of the Isle of Man Government I am pleased to write this introduction to "Moods of Mann" which is a brilliant portfolio of photographs of this lovely Island. The Isle of Man has many locations of quality, charisma and interest. It is true to say that many of the businesses within the island who have supported the production of this book enjoy a similar set of qualities.

The reader will find that the pictures chosen for inclusion in this publication illustrate quite clearly many of the special features that our Island enjoys and how they change in mood depending on the seasons. Sometimes melancholy, sometimes bright but always beautiful and full of wonder.

For those readers who know the Island well this book will remind them of its special qualities and for the reader who does not know the Island so well it cannot help but incite the imagination and interest that is required to 'come and see and enjoy' for oneself.

This book is one that stands alone with its quality of production and contents. It will fill a very real gap in the market place for those searching for the different aspects and 'moods' of Man. I have no doubt that many people will get as much delight and pleasure as I have from browsing through the following pages.

Miles R. Walker,

CHIEF MINISTER. ISLE OF MAN. 1994.

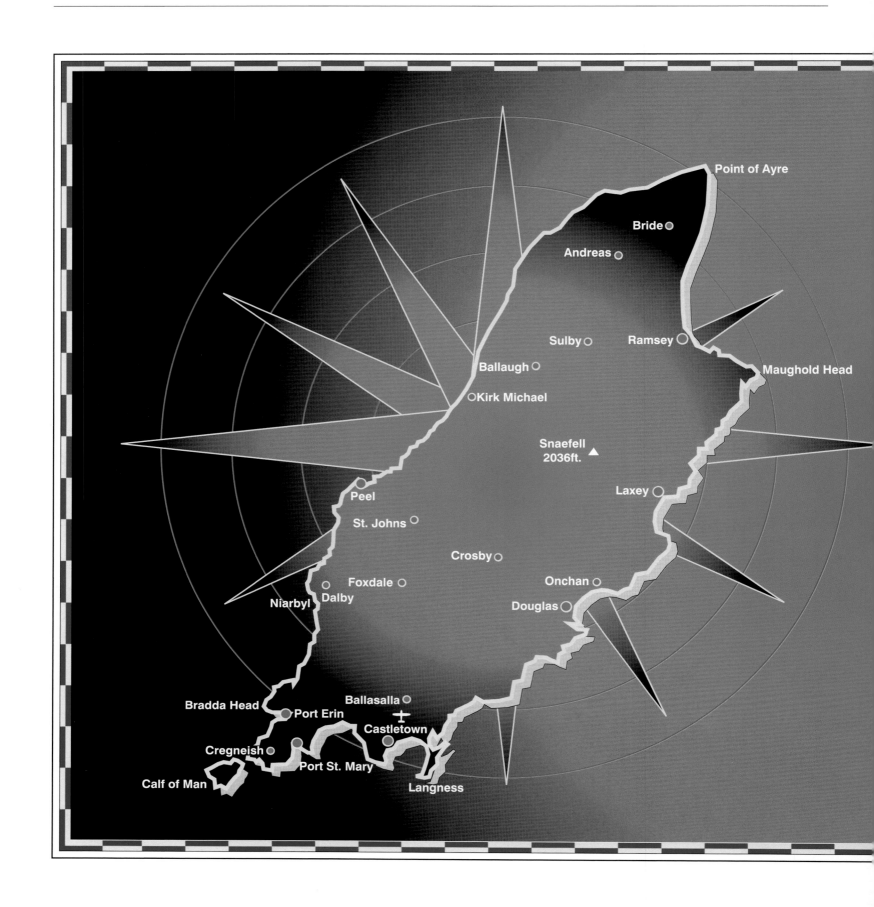

D E M O G R A P H I C S

GEOGRAPHY		DISTANCE FROM: BY AIR:			BY SEA:	
Latitude	54° 3' – 54° 25' N	London Heathrow	276M/ 444km			
Longitude	4° 18' – 4° 47' W	Manchester	109M/ 175km	Heysham	68M/ 109km	
Length	32.5M/ 52.3km	Glasgow	125M/ 200km	Liverpool	83M/ 134km	
Width	13.5M/ 21.73km	Liverpool	87M/ 140km	Belfast	90M/ 144km	
Highest peak Snaefell – 2,036ft/ 620m		Belfast	71M/ 114km	Dublin	92M/ 148km	
		Dublin	84M/ 135km	Ardrossan	114M/ 184km	

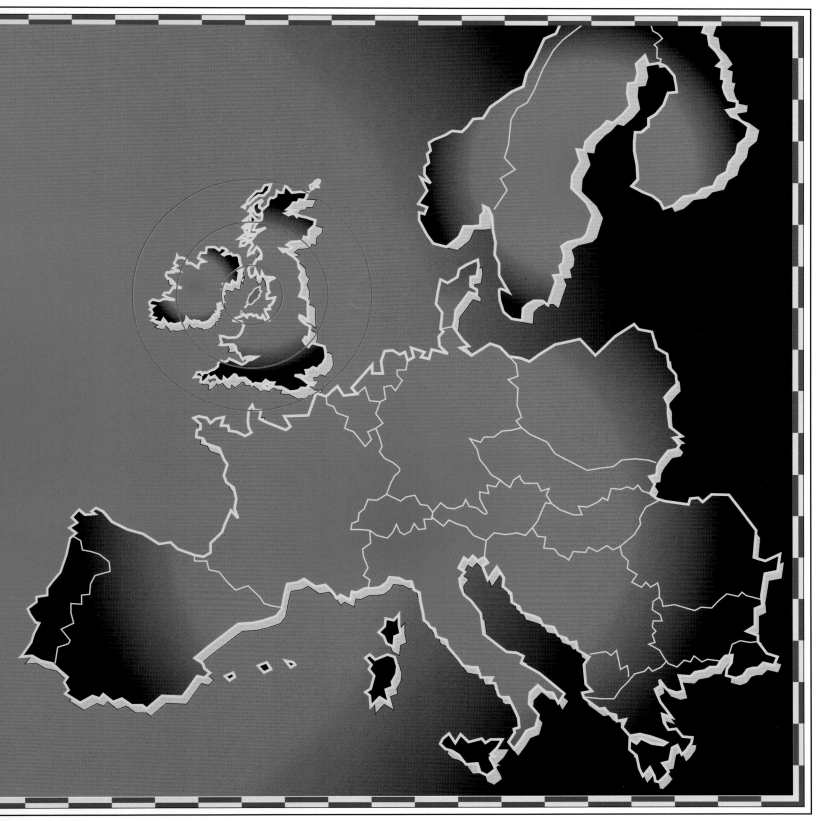

CLIMATE – averages per year:

Sunshine	1,543 hours
Rainfall	871mm

POPULATION and HOUSING
(1991 Census)

Males	33,693
Females	36,095
	Total 69,788

Electorate (1993)	51,575
Total number of homes	27,316
Average house price (1993)	£81,903

FISHING
(1991)

Shellfish	tonnage landed 3,496
Herring/ mackerel and	
other white fish	tonnage landed 1,066

AGRICULTURE
(1993)

Land under crops	12,491 acres
Hay and grassland	65,221 acres
Rough grazing and other	37,613 acres
Cattle (all types) total	32,300
Poultry	56,763
Sheep and lambs	154,065
Horses	1,283

THE PAST

BY MARGERY WEST

Anyone who has seen the midsummer sun rise beyond the Neolithic stones of Cashtal-ny-Ard, or watched a spectacular red sunset silhouette the ruins of Peel castle, will tell you that the Isle of Man is one of those special places which holds a magnetism generated by centuries of legend and belief.

Like other ancient races before them the Celts regarded special places in the lands they occupied as holy. The Isle of Man was one of these and this mystic past has survived to this day.

Nowhere in the world is there such a wealth of ancient archaeology, folklore and history in so small an area. The island's geographical position is also unique, lying as it does at the centre of the British Isles. It is one of those Isles yet it forms no part of the United Kingdom even though the English Sovereign is Lord of Mann.

It is a staunchly independent island with its own parliament (Tynwald) established long before the Westminster Parliament. Similarly its own church was organised before either Canterbury or York.

When stone-age man disappeared from the island, leaving behind his flints, he was followed by Neolithic-man (4,000-2,000 BC) who also left his mark in standing stones and burial cairns.

Then came Bronze-age man, a culture which lasted until the arrival of the Celts around 500 BC. Their remains abound on the island – beautifully made jewellry and weapons, graves, village sites of small round houses, promontory forts, ogham stones, Christian symbols and ruined keeils (churches). It is this Celtic civilisation that forms the basis of Manx culture today.

Far left top: Neolithic stones at Cashtal-yn-Ard.
PHOTOGRAPHED BY MIKE GOLDIE

Other pictures are scenes from re-enactments of the Vikings landing at Peel.

Viking warrior. PHOTOGRAPHED BY NIGEL MALPASS

Sunset over a longship and Viking raiders on the beach. PHOTOGRAPHED BY JOHN C HALL

Left: In 1979 the replica Viking longship 'Odin's Raven' was sailed from Trondheim, Norway, to the Isle of Man in celebration of the island's Millennium.

PHOTOGRAPHED BY IAN COULSON

Below left and right: Intricate stone carvings in the churches and graveyards around the island offer a visual reminder of the island's long history.

PHOTOGRAPHS BY MARTIN CASHEN AND PETER BOYLE

Opposite: St Patrick's Isle. According to legend the first Christian Church was established here. It became fortified as Peel Castle in the Middle Ages and is now linked by a causeway to Peel.

PHOTOGRAPHED BY MARTIN CASHEN

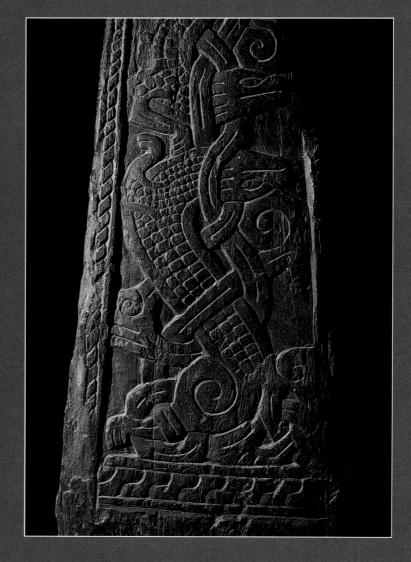

Christianity reached the island in the year 447 when a small group of St Patrick's disciples arrived from Ireland and built the first of many tiny keeils. The site is now known as St Patrick's Isle, today linked by a causeway to the fishing port of Peel.

Myth gave way to the written word when the monks of Rushen Abbey scribed in Latin the island's Domesday Book, *'Cronicon Manniae'*, which begins with the arrival in Mann in 1066 of the legendary Norse ruler Godred Crovan, known to the Manx as King Orry.

Between the 7th and 9th century, Vikings came to plunder and destroy but, by the 10th century they had settled and the island became part of the Scandinavian empire. Norse married Celt and from that union the Manx nation was born. Christianity returned and the Manx church thrived as part of a Norse diocese.

The Viking's greatest legacy however, was the Scandinavian form of government that survives to this day – the oldest form of continuous government in the world.

When the rule of the Norse kings came to an end there was constant war for possession between the Scots and the English. During this turbulent period Peel Castle and Castle Rushen were transformed into formidable fortresses.

Peace came in 1346 when the English defeated the Scots at the battle of Neville's Cross near Durham and conditions on the island became more stable.

From then on the island was ruled by a succession of Lords chosen by the Crown, except during the reign of Elizabeth I. Afraid that her enemies, Spain and France, might make use of the island as a base, she assumed Lordship herself and held it for the rest of her life. Tradition says she presented the clock in the tower at Castle Rushen, still ticking today.

From the beginning of the 15th century it was the Stanleys, Earls of Derby, who became owners of the island, succeeded by their kinsmen, the Dukes of Atholl. This dynasty was to rule for almost four centuries, though few of them ever took up residence.

One who did was James Stanley, 7th Earl of Derby (1627-1651). His name has come down to us today as "The Great Stanley" (Yn Stanlagh Mooar) because of his concern for the welfare of the Manx people.

Stanley was an early entrepreneur, encouraging the Manx to trade knowing the island could never flourish until it built up business with the surrounding nations.

He brought to the island English specialists to teach the impoverished Manx new handicrafts and he helped farmers to improve their breeds of stock.

During the English Civil War it was the same James Stanley who held the island out against Cromwell for seven years, blocking all attempts at invasion. When he left for England to do battle with the Royalists he left his countess (Charlotte) behind to guard the Castle Rushen.

James Stanley was captured at Worcester. Despite pleas for his life Cromwell determined that he should die and gave the order: "Darbie will be tried at Chester and die at Bolton." And so it was.

William Christian (Illiam Dhone) was Governor under the Stanleys and Commandant of the local Militia. He threw in his lot with Parliament, believing it best for his native isle. It was he who

This page: Old mining buildings at sea level below Bradda Head.
PHOTOGRAPHED BY ALEX MADDRELL

Opposite top: The ruins of St German's Cathedral in the grounds of Peel Castle.
PHOTOGRAPHED BY CREATIVE STUDIO

Opposite bottom: The roofless church of St Trinians. According to legend each time the roof was nearly completed the Buggane (a type of goblin) would blow it away.
PHOTOGRAPHED BY MARTIN CASHEN

opened the way for the Roundheads to land at Ramsey and march south to capture Castle Rushen. He remained as Governor until the monarchy was restored, when he was arrested, hurriedly tried for treason and shot at Hango Hill, Castletown. All too late a pardon arrived from King Charles II. Christian's lands and properties were restored to his family. His body was buried in the nave of Malew Church, where his tombstone may be seen today.

It was not until the 18th century that the Manx finally followed The Great Stanley's words of advice; "This island will never succeed till some trade be." They took to smuggling.

To help the economy Tynwald decreed it legal to import free of duty any commodity which could be resold, such as exotic silks and brandy from France, rum from Jamaica.

Fast Manx ships were used for the trade; huge cellars were constructed in harbour towns in which to stock the imports. Even the caves at Port Soderick and Groudle were utilised as warehouses for perfectly legal imports.

Established merchants and amateur entrepreneurs alike made huge profits. The British Government reacted by increasing the numbers of revenue men. But the smuggling went on.

Westminster passed a "Mischief Act" which gave officers of the Royal Navy the right to stop and search any ship. (Young Lieut. William Bligh was one of these officers, later to command *HMS Bounty*).

Finally it was decided the only way to stop the smuggling trade was to repossess the island in the name of the English Crown. The Duke of Atholl was offered tempting compensation, which he agreed and the island was sold by him for £70,000 plus an annuity of £1,740 per year. On July 11th 1765, the Manx flag was hauled down at Castle Rushen. Three volleys were sounded and the standard of Great Britain hoisted. The new Lord of Mann was George III.

During this period the tiny fishing village of Douglas grew into a town with a considerable harbour. By the year 1869 it had ousted Castletown as the capital and the seat of Government moved there. The rule of the Stanleys and Atholls had brought an influx of administrators to the island. These families stayed on to become integrated into the Manx nation, as had previous waves of 'come-overs'.

By the beginning of the 19th century they were joined by a new breed of immigrant – political refugees from Europe, half-pay officers, maintenance men, and others escaping creditors. (Debts incurred in the United Kingdom could not be enforced in Mann).

Over a period of 30 years the island's population doubled from 20,000 to 40,000.

The newcomers brought with them an entirely different style of living. Douglas revelled in gay dinner parties, balls and other social entertainment. A theatre flourished; gentlemen's clubs thrived; an assembly hall was built (Douglas Court House today). New homes sprang up alongside the cottages of the old town. These houses, with their splendid Georgian facades, were clustered around Finch Road, Prospect Hill, Bucks Road and Athol Street, home today of the island's thriving financial sector.

Dominated by Castle Rushen, Castletown was the capital of the island
until around 1869.

PHOTOGRAPHED BY FOLEY VEREKER

Away from the mansion and manor house the life of the working man was far removed from that of the gentry and socialites of Douglas.

In 1823 the herring season failed. The potato harvest was less than half and there was little to substitute for these, the two main items of the Manx diet. Then came the announcement that, to augment the clergy's stipend, a potato tithe was to be imposed of 12 shillings for every acre planted, regardless of the harvest from it.

Riots spread around the island. Martial law was declared, though there were few soldiers to impose it. Castle gates were locked and the Bishop of the day needed a military escort back to Bishopscourt. Eight manxmen were later arrested as ringleaders although only two were brought to trial. The scapegoats were saved from the gallows but were transported for life to Botany Bay.

The tithe was abandoned 10 years later.

Many Manx families never recovered from this tragic period of privation and resolutely set their sights on the New World.

By the middle of the 19th century the flow of Manx emigrants was gathering momentum as good news reached them from the early pioneers. Desperate for a better life families took their leave of cottages that had been home for generations.

Miners sought new jobs in the gold and diamond mines of South Africa and Australia. Farmers made for the lush pastures of New Zealand or the wide spaces of America. Many prospered and made their mark in their adopted countries.

Manx emigrants played a large part in founding the city of Cleveland, Ohio. In fact it was given the name "Manx capital of America". Two generations ago, there were 30,000 Manx descendants in that city, two thirds the population at that time in their native isle. Today Cleveland is the headquarters of the North American Manx Association, which donated the Cleveland gold medal, awarded annually at the Manx Music Festival.

Hango Hill overlooking Castletown Bay, Site of the execution of William Christian (Illiam Dhone) in 1663.

PHOTOGRAPHED BY RICK TOMLINSON

Towards the close of the 19th century there came a giant leap forward in the fortunes of Mann.

A regular steamer link with the mainland had been established as early as 1830 by the Isle of Man Steam Packet Company. There had been great rejoicing when the Manx saw their own three-leg symbol on the paddle box of 'Mona's Isle' preserved today in the Manx Museum.

It was the beginning of a fleet that was to become the successful company of today, believed to be the oldest continuously operated passenger line in the world.

This steamer link was the early beginning of the tourist trade that was to reverse the fortunes of the Manx nation by the end of the century. In fact it could be said that the development of the Steam Packet fleet put a new value on every inch of the island.

Douglas teemed with life in the season. There were horse trams, cable lifts, amusement halls and arcades, circuses, a waxworks, bandstands, minstrel and pierrot shows. The Palace ballroom was built, the finest and biggest in Europe and there were ballrooms at Derby Castle and Falcon Cliff. Top vaudeville artists appeared at the island's two music halls.

Such was the boom in Manx tourism that during the last summer of peace in 1913, the Steam Packet's fleet of fifteen ships carried more than a million passengers. The First World War changed all that – and Manx tourism has not yet been able to turn back the clock.

Eleven of the Steam Packet vessels were commandeered by the Admiralty. Only the four smallest steamers were left to serve the Isle of Man. They carried vital supplies to the island but their passengers were mainly the 28,000 enemy aliens who were to spend the war behind the barbed wire of two vast internment camps. Hoteliers and boarding-house landladies went bankrupt.

The tourist industry revived between the wars, though never to the same extent. A growing number of enthusiasts did come to the island for the Tourist Trophy motorcycle races which grew through the twenties and thirties to international status. Today, the June TT fortnight is still the biggest tourist attraction.

World War Two brought a similar decline to that of 1914 and again the island became an enormous interment camp.

In the 1960's, when the island's population had reached a low of 47,000, the Government launched a policy to attract new residents. The inducement was low income tax, no death duties, nil inheritance tax, no property tax and no capital gains tax.

Previous Spread: Castletown market square
in Victorian times.
PHOTOGRAPHED BY DONALD GELLION

Top Left: Steam Power earlier this century.
PHOTOGRAPHED BY MRS. M. KINNIN

Bottom Left: Douglas seafront during the heyday
of tourism.
PHOTOGRAPH FROM THE KEIG COLLECTION

Top: Fish sellers on the quay at Douglas.
PHOTOGRAPHED BY W. ROYSTON

Right: Herring drifters alongside the North Quay, Douglas.
PHOTOGRAPH FROM THE KEIG COLLECTION

The policy succeeded. Today the population has touched the target of 70,000 with consequential benefit to the Manx economy.

More recently, the Government set out to further benefit the economy by expanding the island into a profitable international trading zone. New business incentives were promised to ensure that the island never again had to depend for its livelihood on tourism, fishing and agriculture alone.

This sustainable growth has developed in areas of high technology industry; financial services; insurance; banking and ship management. Today there is no need for young people to seek work away from home – the island is close to achieving nil unemployment. It has a new future.

There is however still plenty of space to breathe in Mann's 227 square miles. The countryside is unspoilt; glens and mountains offer peace and solitude.

And there are still mythical sunrises in the east and breathtaking red sunsets in the west.

Below: Creigneish village. Today maintained as a living museum.
PHOTOGRAPHED BY RICK TOMLINSON

Right: The narrow streets of Peel.
PHOTOGRAPHED BY EYE OF MAN/ MICHAEL THOMPSON

PHOTOGRAPHED BY RICK TOMLINSON

PHOTOGRAPHED BY JEREMY PAUL

THE ISLAND AND THE SEA

BY DAVID M WILSON

Sunlight on a tranquil sea.

The Isle of Man lies in the northern part of the Irish Sea. It sees all that goes on; it observes its neighbours and checks their comings and goings. In its position lies its strength. The sea provides and has provided for centuries, both wealth and protection. Viking chieftains, Scottish kings, English lords and French smugglers have all used its position as a base for their operations. The sea provides food; cod, mackerel and particularly herring were long central to the island's economy. The sea and its ally the mist (the cloak of the benign wizard Manannan) kept away enemies. The sea gave independence, provided for easy trade and brought tourists. The sea was policed by powerful nations with navies, customs cutters and privateers. Passage from the island to the neighbouring countries was strictly controlled and strangers were not always welcome. The coast itself is often inhospitable – it is no accident that the Royal National Lifeboat Institution was founded on the island. But, bathed in light on a bright summer day, the Island acts as a magnet for all those who live around the Irish Sea.

Islands have an irresistible fascination. Sea, sky, light and colour combine to heighten perception and stimulate imagination. Islands represent the freedom of childhood holidays, release from the stuffiness of towns and nostalgia for a free and independent life. T.E.Brown, the Manx national poet, captures it in his soft native dialect:

Now the beauty of the thing when childher play is

The terrible wonderful length the day is.

Up you jumps, and out in the sun

And you fancy the day will never be done;

And you're chasin' the bumbees hummin' so cross

In the hot sweet air among the gorse,

Or gat'rin' bluebells, or lookin' for eggs,

Or peltin' the ducks with their yalla legs,

Or climbin' and nearly breakin' your skulls,

Or shoutin' for divilment after the gulls,

Or thinkin' of nothin', but down at the tide

Singin' out for the happy you feel inside.

Right: Cool waters shaded by Ballaglass Glen.
PHOTOGRAPHED BY JOHN NEIL

Below: South Barrule reflected in an upland pool.
PHOTOGRAPHED BY CREATIVE STUDIO

That islands – as any community – can be inward looking is self-evident; but no island can be totally self-sufficient. Ultimately the island-dweller must set out on a sea voyage.

The Isle of Man is as contradictory as any other island – perhaps more so than most. The grey suits of the business world of Douglas give way at weekends to wet-suits or climber's shirts. Twenty minutes from the banking halls are bare uninhabited moors, home only to hen-harriers and larks; or you can catch the tide and head for an evening's fishing.

For much of the year the Isle of Man is a private place, celebrating its own festivals and living its own life. But there are other sides to the island. It is also a Mecca to motor-bike road-racers. Enthusiasts come from all over the world to watch the races and to show off their own lovingly-kept machines. At other times jazz sessions or chamber music are the loudest sounds. In summer, some tourists reflect a rapidly fading northern English tradition of holidays on the beach. Others, French, German and

Far left: Heather carpeted hillside to the south of Cronkdoo.
PHOTOGRAPHED BY MICHAEL THOMPSON - EYE OF MAN

Left: The Arboretum at St John's.
PHOTOGRAPHED BY JOHN C. HALL

Below: Maughold Head and the island's east coast.
PHOTOGRAPHED BY RICK TOMLINSON

even Japanese bring an international flavour. Like the sea around it the island is never still; it has its moods and its transformations.

Any country is formed by its geology, its geography and its history. The island is dominated by its upland slate massif, itself divided by the deep central valley which joins Douglas to Peel.

The northern section of this upland region is the higher, rising to the mountain of Snaefell at 2036 feet (620m) which may be seen from the coasts of Cumbria or Ireland on most days. To the south the hills roll more gently to the peak of South Barrule at 1585 feet (483m).

To the north of the mountains a plain of gravel ridges and sand dunes rises over 330 feet (100m) above sea level before dropping to a wild heathland and a brutally scoured gravel beach at the Point of Ayre.

Between Ballaugh and Sulby lies the wild and hardly inhabited wetland area of the Curraghs. Its sodden, peaty fields are home to a few sheep and cattle (including the local Manx strain of four-horned brown-coated Loghtan sheep), while its abundant wildlife and flora includes great sweeps of marsh orchids with their attendant butterflies.

The southern plain is underlain by limestone which provides the distinctive grey building stone for much of the area.

The ancient native vegetation has almost entirely disappeared and modern tree plantation in certain upland areas has been less than sympathetic. But in the valleys, on the lowlands and in the deep glens, lush deciduous vegetation closes in to give a dappled appearance to those areas that remain uncultivated. Inland from the northern town of Ramsey, the grazing cattle and crowned trees resemble nothing so much as English parkland. The glens (seventeen of which are in public

Above: Misty sea at Niarbyl Point.
PHOTOGRAPHED BY SIMON PARK

Right: Barregarrow.
PHOTOGRAPHED BY FOLEY VEREKER

ownership) are a major natural feature of the island and were in Victorian times much exploited for the tourist industry, often being planted with exotic trees, paved and provided with rustic furnishing and shelters. More recently they have lost this function but are still carefully managed to ensure that the tree cover and the fast running rivers which originally formed the glens themselves are made accessible to walkers. The turf banks of many of the roadsides are filled with wild flowers, from the appearance of primroses in springtime until the more exotic fuschia of summer challenges the gorse. T.E.Brown, bowed down by the life of a schoolmaster in Bristol, remembered these colours and their attendant wonders:

I'm here at Clifton, grinding at the mill
My feet for thrice nine barren years have trod;
But there are rocks and waves at Scarlett still
And gorse runs riot in Glen Chass – thank God!

Alert, I seek exactitude of rule,
I step, and square my shoulders with the squad;
But there are blaeberries on old Barrule
And Langness has its heather still – thank God!

What then of the people?

Like most who live by the sea they are a mongrel crew, a nation which becomes more mixed every year as new industries and nationalities settle in the island. But this was always so. The original Stone Age inhabitants were incomers, related to the people around the Irish Sea. At the beginning of its recorded history a Gaelic-speaking people lived on Man, a people whose language was basically that of the Irish.

They were invaded and settled by Norse Vikings – most romantic of all seafarers – towards the end of the ninth century. These newcomers introduced their own language, but only to the upper echelons of society. An under-class survived who spoke Gaelic and who occasionally married with the Norse incomers. These were the people who emerged at the end of the Norse period with an intact language which adapted itself to the softer Gaelic of the Scottish rulers who followed.

Below: The rugged southern coastline.

PHOTOGRAPHED BY JOHN C. HALL

The Norse left many traces in the Island. The present name of the bishopric (Sodor and Man) refers to those very isles Magnus ceded to Norway, a see founded from the Norwegian archdiocese across the ocean in Trondheim. Throughout the island place names reflect the Norse occupation of nearly four hundred years. Such names as Snaefell ('snow-mountain'), Dalby ('settlement in the valley'), Langness ('long headland').

The rough sea-going Vikings of legend left remnants of their culture; crosses ornamented in Norse decorative styles and inscribed with the runic alphabet of the North, occasionally depicting Scandinavian legend; burial mounds which enshrined the bodies of the very first settlers; a system of land-holding and symbols of the authority which upheld the law in the beginnings of two fine castles. Chiefly, however, it left its governing assembly – Tynwald – which celebrated its millennium in 1979. The open-air meeting of the legislature on Tynwald Hill in St John's each

Right: The lighthouse at Langness Point. The southern-most tip of the island.

PHOTOGRAPHED BY FOLEY VEREKER

*Above: The Tower of Refuge was built by Sir William Hillary as a haven
for the many sailors who were shipwrecked on the rocks at the
entrance to Douglas Harbour. In storm conditions they would shelter in
the tower until rescued. Hillary later founded the
Royal National Lifeboat Institution.*

PHOTOGRAPHED BY RICK TOMLINSON

year on 5th July reflects the recorded customs of the Island in the Middle Ages and its roots in the politics of far-away Scandinavian nations.

The Scottish kings who replaced the Scandinavian rulers brought in administrators who took as their right the land and privileges of their predecessors. They also brought trouble in the form of disputed claims to the throne of Man, particularly after Magnus Godredson, the last Norse claimant to the Manx throne, was defeated by a Scottish army at the Battle of Ronaldsway (the site of the present airport) in 1275.

In the nineteenth century a different use of the sea changed the Manx economy. More reliable sea communication encouraged the island's lead mining industry which peaked in the 1880's, only to die by 1920. But it was the tourist industry that remoulded the outward appearance of the Isle of Man, that built its promenades and boarding houses.

Then once again the Manx economy changed. The sea voyage (often unpleasantly rough) became less adventurous and in the 1960's, the Mediterranean package holiday became a cheaper and more attractive option. Tourists are still attracted to the island but now offshore financial services connected by air and fax line have replaced the great adventure of the sea.

The Isle of Man – infinitely adaptable – has survived and flourishes, as it always has done, in the spirit of the merchant adventurer.

But its beauty remains;

But Bradda still has lichens worth the seeing

And thunder in her caves – thank God!

T.E.BROWN.

Above: The Fisherman's Cottage, Niarbyl.

PHOTOGRAPHED BY FOLEY VEREKER

Bottom: Castletown Promenade from across the bay.

PHOTOGRAPHED BY JOHN NEIL

Left: Peel Castle on St Patrick's Isle. First mentioned in history as the original site of Christian worship on the island, the castle was fortified in the middle ages.

PHOTOGRAPHED BY JOHN C. HALL

Above: Herring has been landed on the island for hundreds of years and along with potatoes once formed the staple diet of the people. Today Manx kippers are a speciality renowned the world over.

PHOTOGRAPHED BY TONY LAKIN

Maughold Lighthouse.

PHOTOGRAPHED BY RICK TOMLINSON

Above: Sheep trek along the path on the western slopes of
Cronk Ny Areey Laa − 'The Hill of the Rising Day'.
PHOTOGRAPHED BY TONY LAKIN

Right: Port Erin, a favourite haunt of the summer visitor,
changes dramatically in the winter gales.
PHOTOGRAPHED BY ROSEMARY GREENWOOD

Above: The view from Mull Hill looking across Port Erin to South Barrule.

PHOTOGRAPHED BY ROSEMARY GREENWOOD

Right: Arbory Street, Castletown. Part of the old town.

PHOTOGRAPHED BY JEREMY PAUL

Above: Aerial view of Douglas.

PHOTOGRAPHED BY RICK TOMLINSON

Right: 'Smoking chimneys' – Douglas.

PHOTOGRAPHED BY CREATIVE STUDIO

Fishing boats tied outside the British Hotel on the North Quay, Douglas.
A sight that has changed little in a hundred years.
PHOTOGRAPHED BY FOLEY VEREKER

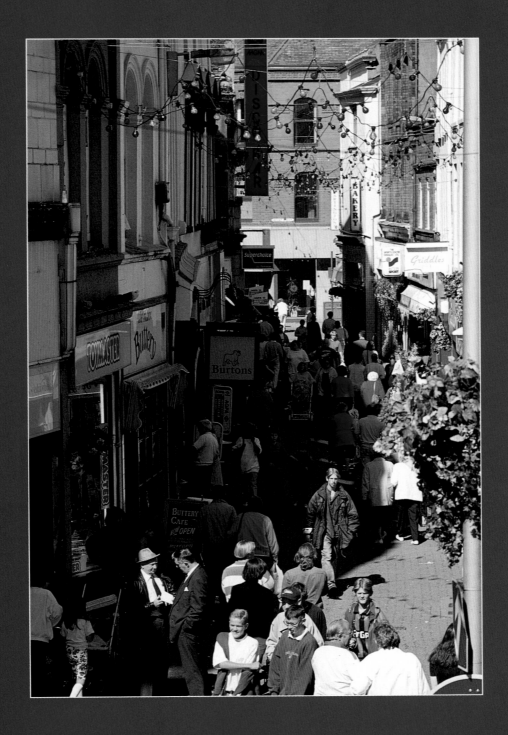

Strand Street, The bustling shopping centre of Douglas.

PHOTOGRAPHED BY RICK TOMLINSON

*During busy summer weekends visiting yachts lie alongside
local fishing boats in Port St Mary.*

PHOTOGRAPHED BY RICK TOMLINSON

*St John's Church on the ancient field
of Tynwald.*

PHOTOGRAPHED BY RICK TOMLINSON

*The Legislative Buildings, Douglas, seat of the Isle of Man
Government.*

PHOTOGRAPHED BY ROSEMARY GREENWOOD

*Above: Fishing boats in Port St Mary. Depending on the time of year
the catch is principally scallops and queenies and
in the summer months, herring.*
PHOTOGRAPHED BY FOLEY VEREKER

Right: The restful summer gardens on the promenade, Douglas.
PHOTOGRAPHED BY TONY LAKIN

Left: Violent seas close the Shore Road, Gansey, during a winter gale. Patrons of the Shore Hotel sometimes have to stay longer than anticipated.
PHOTOGRAPHED BY JOHN NEIL

Above: Clearing the road after the storm.
PHOTOGRAPHED BY MARTIN CASHEN

Top: Breaking wave.
PHOTOGRAPHED BY JOHN ATKINSON

Left: An easterly gale lashes Port St Mary threatening damage to the fishing boats tied to the breakwater.
PHOTOGRAPHED BY DR BEN HEXTALL

Next Page: Lady of Mann off Douglas Head.
PHOTOGRAPHED BY RICK TOMLINSON

*Port St Mary lifeboat. The island has five lifeboats on station which
form an integral part of the cover for the Irish Sea.*

PHOTOGRAPHED BY RICK TOMLINSON

*Air-sea rescue training on the island's steep shores with 22 Squadron,
based at RAF Valley on Anglesey, North Wales.*

PHOTOGRAPHED BY ALAN WATTERSON

*An extreme high tide combined with gale force winds whips up the sea
outside the Nautical Museum in Castletown.*

Photographed by J.M. Cole

Left: Mist (Manannan's Cloak) shrouds boats at Derbyhaven.
PHOTOGRAPHED BY ROSEMARY GREENWOOD

Right: Fishing boats await the incoming tide at Port Erin.
PHOTOGRAPHED BY ROSEMARY GREENWOOD

Below: Point of Ayre lighthouse, one of five around the island's coast.
PHOTOGRAPHED BY GUS GREGORY

Sulby Reservoir surrounded by the broad expanse of the unspoilt countryside.

PHOTOGRAPHED BY RICK TOMLINSON

Above: Mooragh Park.

PHOTOGRAPHED BY EYE OF MAN - MICHAEL THOMPSON

Right: Winter landscape.

PHOTOGRAPHED BY TONY LAKIN

NEXT PAGE: PHOTOGRAPHED BY SIMON PARK

On the slip at Ramsey, the last working shipyard on the island.

PHOTOGRAPHED BY ROSEMARY GREENWOOD

The commercial wharf in Ramsey harbour.

PHOTOGRAPHED BY ROSEMARY GREENWOOD

Bay-ny-Carrickey looking towards Langness Point.

PHOTOGRAPHED BY TONY LAKIN

*Trawler racing at Port St Mary attracts competitors from all the
island ports as well as from further afield.*

PHOTOGRAPHED BY JOHN C. HALL

Left: Near Kirk Michael.

PHOTOGRAPHED BY ROSEMARY GREENWOOD

Above: The inner harbour at Douglas and the well-known goose which thinks it's a swan.

PHOTOGRAPHED BY TONY LAKIN

*Below: A fine example of early 20th Century architecture, the airport
has developed to meet the needs of the modern air traveller
whilst still retaining its character.*

PHOTOGRAPHED BY RICK TOMLINSON

*Right: Some buildings have not been so well preserved – a ruined farm
building near Port Lewellyn.*

PHOTOGRAPHED BY MICHAEL THOMPSON - EYE OF MAN

The seasons of Mann.

PHOTOGRAPHED BY SIMON PARK

Hotels dominate the promenade at Port Erin.

PHOTOGRAPHED BY ROSEMARY GREENWOOD

Top: An original doorway to a fisherman's cottage.
Above: Interior of St German's cathedral in Peel Castle.

<small>Photographed by Rosemary Greenwood</small>

Evening trawl.

PHOTOGRAPHED BY RICK TOMLINSON

The Herring Tower at Langness.

PHOTOGRAPHED BY ROSEMARY GREENWOOD

The Burroo off the Calf of Man, known locally as 'the drinking dragon'.

PHOTOGRAPHED BY TONY LAKIN

Spray covers the Thusla tower in the Sound.

PHOTOGRAPHED BY TONY LAKIN

*Above left: Traditional Manx
stone work.*

PHOTOGRAPHED BY ROSEMARY GREENWOOD

*Above right: The old farm at Cregneish.
Today the whole village is maintained
as a living museum.*

PHOTOGRAPHED BY FOLEY VEREKER

*Right: Dramatic light illuminates a
restored cottage on the Howe.*

PHOTOGRAPHED BY ROSEMARY GREENWOOD

Right: Rolling farmland.

PHOTOGRAPHED BY SIMON PARK

Bottom: Bradda Head at sunset.

PHOTOGRAPHED BY MICHAEL THOMPSON - EYE OF MAN

Derbyhaven.

PHOTOGRAPHED BY FOLEY VEREKER

Early morning - Peel Harbour.

PHOTOGRAPHED BY TRICIA CRAIG

*The famous Laxey Wheel. The 'Lady Isabella' - designed to lift water
1500 feet from the nearby mines.*

PHOTOGRAPHED BY MICHAEL THOMPSON - EYE OF MAN

*There are many explanations for the tail-less Manx cat. One recounts that they were
the last to board Noah's Ark and the door was closed on their tails!
In fact the Manx cat is a natural mutation and is found in other parts of the world.*

PHOTOGRAPHED BY RICK TOMLINSON

Tynwald Ceremony in July. Each year the government meet at this ancient site, a tradition which has endured for over 1000 years.

PHOTOGRAPHED BY CREATIVE STUDIO

Her Royal Highness, the Princess Royal at the Tynwald Ceremony.

PHOTOGRAPHED BY NIGEL MALPASS

*Douglas Promenade by night, compared by some to the Bay of Naples
for its beauty, if not its temperature. Visited by millions of tourists from
the late nineteenth century to the present day.*

PHOTOGRAPHED BY PETER BOYCE

Castletown harbour, guarded by the ancient fortress of Castle Rushen.

PHOTOGRAPHED BY CREATIVE STUDIO

Above: Chapel in winter - Peel.
PHOTOGRAPHED BY J.R. SHIMMIN

Right: Cornelly Mines.
PHOTOGRAPHED BY ROSEMARY GREENWOOD

Above: Old farm buildings at the Howe, Douglas Head.

Right: Moon over water.

Left: The Mountains of Mourne in Ireland, seen here from the beach at Port Erin are at least 50 miles away.

Photographed by Rick Tomlinson

Above: 'Sea Bird'.

Photographed by Tony Lakin

THE PEOPLE

BY TERRY CRINGLE

In the Manx General Election campaign of 1971 one of the great concerns in the Island at the time, among the native Manx at least, was the large numbers of so-called New Residents who seemed to be arriving daily, anxious to test the Manx Government's diagnosis that living under the Isle of Man's easy-going tax regime would be good for their wealth.

Certainly there was cause for concern. The new-comers were well-to-do. They forced up property and other prices. They were also seen as introducing an alien culture into the Island and, as persons not of Manx birth, a threat to the very survival of the Manx nation.

The pressures on the island's social fabric were indeed severe, so much so that Manx nationalist feeling was running high and showing a violent cutting edge. A secret organisation called Fo Halloo was producing inflammatory pamphlets about political corruption. Its members would stalk the night, daubing Manx nationalist slogans on walls and sometimes on the houses of New Residents with rather too high a local profile.

It was against this background that one candidate − a good Manxman − was asked by a member of the audience what he thought about the dreadful influx of English tax dodgers. He replied, with all the blunt honesty of the soldier: "What we should remember is that if it wasn't for the English coming over the Manx would be back in the trees."

He didn't win the election and Manx politics lost the services of a brave man. That remark is now almost completely forgotten but there was much in what he said.

What kind of people would the native Manx have become if there had never been any new blood, new ideas and the sort of new conflicts that can be good for the development of humankind?

Immigration on the whole has been good for us, even if it has made it difficult to define exactly what a Manxman or woman now is.

Certainly there can be few Manx who can say they are truly Manx, if that means having an unbroken ancestral line going back to the Vikings. Today most people living on the island are not Manx-born. This was not always the case but, certainly in the years since the Second World war, the number of non-Manx has been growing steadily.

The balance was finally shown to have tilted in favour of the non-Manx when the results of the Island's 1991 population census were announced. The percentage majority of non-Manx had inched just over 50%. It was only less than a percentage point difference. But it was a moment of truth for the Manx people.

For the first time in their history, as far as is known, they had become a minority in their own land.

But it was always going to happen, just as the non-Manx majority is likely to increase in the years to come. We have only to look at the island's history to see that 'New Residents' have been arriving on its shores for at least 10 centuries.

It was not until 1765 when ownership of the Island was "revested" in the Crown, a situation which applies today, that the first of the New Residents with whom we are more familiar today began to arrive.

Digging for bait.
Photographed by Michael Thompson - Eye of Man

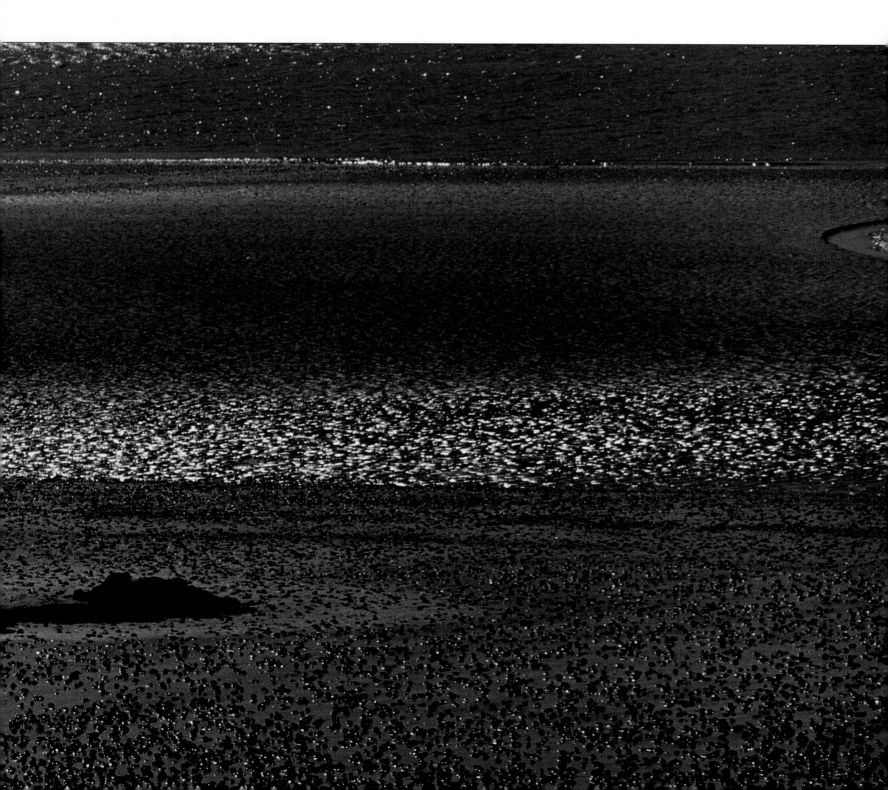

One such was David Robertson a British customs officer stationed in Douglas for a time in the 18th century. He eventually left the Island but in 1791 returned for a leisure visit. He was, in effect, one of the Island's first tourists. The Grand Tour through Europe was a rather risky business at the time because of the French Revolution, so people with an urge to travel began to explore the British Isles.

Mr Robertson chose the place where he had worked and in 1794 his *"A Tour Through the Isle of Man"* was published in London, so it is likely that he was also one of the first to write a travel book.

Mr Robertson tells us that even in those days the island had a reputation as a tax haven. "Of late years several English farmers, sinking under the accumulated taxes of their own country, have retired to a land as yet exempt from such oppression. Here they enjoy peace and abundance while the success attending their agricultural labours seems at length to have roused the Manx from their lethargy."

Right: Sheep take precedence along the country lanes.
PHOTOGRAPHED BY MICHAEL THOMPSON - EYE OF MAN

Below: Knowledgeable discussion at an Agricultural Show.
PHOTOGRAPHED BY CREATIVE STUDIO

All in all Mr Robertson took a dim view of the Manx people. "Indolence is a prominent feature of the Manks character..." He talks of their "superstitious delusions" and "the harmless but sullen lunatics who so frequently distress the feeling mind in this country." He also accused the wealthy and more sophisticated Manx of being "haughty in their deportment and illiberal in their prejudices."

Mr Robertson has much more to say about the Isle of Man and the Manx but there is no need to repeat it here. He has made his point. And he is unlikely to have shown himself back in the island after his book was published.

The Isle of Man continued to exist without income tax until 1918 and even when it was brought in it was levied at enviably low levels. Slowly, as the 20th century wore on, hard-headed businessmen from the north of England saw the advantages of moving themselves and their money into the island's handsome country house.

There were not many of them but they were all part of the continuing and intensifying English infiltration.

The first deliberate attempt to promote the island as a haven for wealthy New Residents is usually credited to the

Left: Herring being gutted before smoking into 'kippers'.
PHOTOGRAPHED BY ROSEMARY GREENWOOD

Right: A variety of fish are caught by the local fishing fleet.
PHOTOGRAPHED BY CREATIVE STUDIO

Below Left: Cleaning the catch on board.
PHOTOGRAPHED BY ALEX MADDRELL

Below Right: Herring have been smoked on the island
for hundreds of years.
PHOTOGRAPHED BY CREATIVE STUDIO

The island's professionals.

LEFT: PHOTOGRAPHED BY ROSEMARY GREENWOOD

RIGHT: PHOTOGRAPHED BY ALEX MADDRELL

BOTTOM LEFT: PHOTOGRAPHED BY ROSEMARY GREENWOOD

BOTTOM RIGHT: PHOTOGRAPHED BY MIKE GOLDIE

decision of Tynwald, around 1962, to abolish surtax on the Island. The decision immediately caught the eyes of the rich, tax-burdened English. The invasion was well and truly on.

Perhaps the real credit for perceiving that this was a way of strengthening the Manx economy should go to a man called J.R.Quayle, a one-time chairman of the Isle of Man Bank. His annual report was not only a message of comfort to shareholders. It was also something of a 'state of the nation' address.

In his 1944 annual report he said too little attention was being paid to the value of people coming to live in retirement on the Isle of Man. He told the Manx Government it should avoid increasing taxes because the retired English were "an unquestioned asset to the business community and to the Island as a whole... The warmest welcome should be extended to them, every encouragement should be offered, and there should be avoided, as far as circumstances permit, taxation at such levels as might not only discourage prospective residents but incline those already here to leave."

Needless to say, JR was a Manxman.

And so, one way or another, the English are now in the majority in the Isle of Man. There are still rumblings of nationalist discontent, there is still concern for the survival of the Manx identity, institutions and culture, but this is no longer as serious

as it was a quarter-of-a-century ago. English intervention in the affairs of the Isle of Man has made the Island more prosperous and young Manx people can now find jobs at home rather than having to move away.

Also, it was the Manx themselves who allowed their native language to be eradicated by English usage in the 19th century. Fortunately Manx Gaelic has been brought back from the brink. There are now hundreds of enthusiasts for the old language, many of whom are what are still called non-Manx.

Similarly the English – and the other nationalities that are arriving all the time – are often only too anxious to participate in the life of the island and they are often more vociferous in its defence than the Manx.

When you listen to Manx Radio today and hear interviews with people who have brought credit on the Isle of Man by their achievements in sport or the arts or other fields of endeavour, you will hear them speak in the accents of Manchester or London, as much if not more than in the accents of Peel or Port Erin.

But we native Manx are perfectly happy to acknowledge them as good Manxmen and women.

'Fun Run'.
PHOTOGRAPHED BY BRIAN GOLDIE

Left: Children out of school can enjoy the freedom of the countryside.
PHOTOGRAPHED BY CREATIVE STUDIO

Above: Time to reminisce.
PHOTOGRAPHED BY MICHAEL THOMPSON - EYE OF MAN

Left: The many local fairs and festivals encourage involvement from all ages.

PHOTOGRAPHED BY MARTIN CASHEN

Below: Fishermen enjoy a joke at the end of the day.

PHOTOGRAPHED BY MR R.E.BALL

"The leisure activities of the countryside are to be found within a few minutes of leaving a busy office."

PHOTOGRAPHED BY MICHAEL THOMPSON - EYE OF MAN

Relaxation on the island can take very different forms!

LEFT: PHOTOGRAPHED BY ALEX MADDRELL

RIGHT: PHOTOGRAPHED BY RICK TOMLINSON

The surrounding sea provides a range of activities for those who enjoy getting wet!

LEFT: PHOTOGRAPHED BY DR BEN HEXTALL

ABOVE, ABOVE RIGHT AND BELOW: PHOTOGRAPHED BY RICK TOMLINSON

PHOTOGRAPHED BY MICHAEL THOMPSON

THE SEASONS

BY JOHN KITTO

Winter

Island winters are wet and inclined to be windy but they are not cold, at least not often. Insulated from extremes by the warm encircling waters of the Gulf Stream, the island experiences between thirty and sixty days of ground frost and around twenty-two days of air frost a year. The daily temperature seldom drops much below 5° C (40°F) while snow or sleet occur on about eighteen days in the year.

An old Manx song describes the town of Ramsey as 'shining by the sea' confirming the sunshine pattern; the north is the sunniest, the south the windiest.

Although many of the old Manx customs have died out over the years, by no means moribund is the New Year's Eve ritual of the Qualtagh or First Foot. Some people still confess to staying

Winter skyline.

PHOTOGRAPHED BY CREATIVE STUDIO

up until long after midnight waiting in some anxiety for the first person not of the household – the Qualtagh – to come to the door, hoping that he will be a dark man. If he has a proper understanding of his obligations, he will have brought an offering of fuel, bread and salt, and will repeat the old rhyme in Manx in which he will wish the recipient:

'A Merry Christmas and a very good year

Luck and health to the whole household,

Life and merriment to you that are living together,

Peace and love between man and woman.'

Should snow arrive in reasonable quantities and be matched to sunny weather, Snaefell becomes the destination for 'winter sport' enthusiasts. Never mind that toboggans and sledges are in short supply. Youngsters, hardy in the right places, can be seen shooting down the steep hillside totally out of control on kitchen trays or sheets of polythene.

The island's temperate climate means that as early as January the welcome signs of spring begin to appear. Snowdrops, crocuses and daffodils peep up to welcome the new year.

Above: Christmas lights at Ballacraine farm on the TT course.
PHOTOGRAPHED BY MIKE GOLDIE

Right: A winter storm pounds the island's coastline.
PHOTOGRAPHED BY FOLEY VEREKER

Next Pages: An unusual event in Peel. Snow rarely lingers for more than a few days even on the exposed hillsides.
PHOTOGRAPHED BY MIRIAM CRITCHLOW

Spring

Now arrives the most glorious period of the year. Daffodils seem suddenly to bow their slender spikes and trumpet into flower as though from some unspoken command. Soon celandines appear and then, on the hillsides bluebells add a gentian haze over the dead bracken or lay a carpet over the fallen leaves in the woods.

Mountain hares perform mad antics on the open heathland, some still piebald, having left unshed part of their winter coats before donning their summer dun colouring. A glowing pair of eyes caught in the car headlights gives notice that a polecat ferret, one of nature's razor-toothed bandits, is on the prowl, ready to feast upon young rabbit or struggling fledgling.

The bird song becomes less strident as demanding screeches from young in the nest spur both parents to greater efforts.

The tourist season begins too. The Easter hockey festival brings teams from all over England as do the athletics, football and rugby festivals. The traditional Manx Music festival –

The Guild – provides a whole week of music, drama and folk dancing competitions.

Then the trickle of visitors suddenly turns into a torrent as the motorcycle fans descend on the Island. Hotels, guest houses, apartments, private houses, camp sites and even some secluded sandy coves fill up overnight. It is TT fortnight again and motorcycles are parked for miles along the promenades and outside every guest house. Pubs and bars slough off their gentle winter ways as they are invaded by the young (and not-so-young) clad in their colourful leathers.

Despite the roar of high performance engines from racing motorcycles, May and June remain the most beautiful months in the year. Away from the road circuits the countryside is as peaceful as ever and, on the high fells, sky larks maintain a running commentary in bird song.

Late in June the motorcycles depart and the island drifts briefly back to sleep while it waits for the summer visitors to arrive.

Right: A moorhens nest.
PHOTOGRAPHED BY T.S. MARTIN

*Below: Colours of spring carpet
the countryside.*
PHOTOGRAPHED BY FOLEY VEREKER

Left: Spring greenery.

Photographed by Rick Tomlinson

Top Right: The Gaiety. A late Victorian theatre that has remained virtually intact.

Bottom Right: An ancient setting for dancers at the Peel music festival.

Photographed by Rosemary Greenwood

*The Isle of Man TT. For two weeks the island echoes
to the thunder of motor-bikes.*

ABOVE PHOTOGRAPHED BY CREATIVE STUDIO

BELOW: PHOTOGRAPHED BY TONY LAKIN

BOTTOM: PHOTOGRAPHED BY ISLAND PHOTOGRAPHICS

RIGHT: PHOTOGRAPHED BY TONY LAKIN

FAR RIGHT PHOTOGRAPHED BY CREATIVE STUDIO

Summer

However lightly and from whichever quarter the winds may blow, the island benefits from sea breezes that tends to keep it a little too well insulated from the sometimes roasting heatwaves experienced on the adjacent islands.

The average daily temperature for July, August and September is no more than 16°C (60°F). The sea is never really warm, attracting only the hardiest of bathers, but the clear water has great appeal to those who enjoy 'messing about in boats'. Long stretches of sandy beach and rocky coves where fat crabs can be hunted, provide endless entertainment for the young.

Though fewer than in the past, visitors begin to fill up the vacancies in the smaller hotels and guest houses in July, particularly along the promenades of Douglas and Port Erin. Sight-seers in coaches cruise the countryside and holiday window shoppers saunter along the town shopping streets.

Summer entertainments primarily for visitors cover a wide range of sporting activities, theatres, fishing and a variety of motor cycle and car racing events.

Of a more cultural nature is the highly acclaimed Mananan International Festival of Music and the Arts at Port Erin, which draws performers from all over the world.

Although not originally intended as a tourist attraction the Tynwald Day ceremony in early July is probably attended by more visitors than any other event except the TT fortnight. Held on the 12 foot (3.7m) high Tynwald Hill at St Johns, it is not just the stage on which is annually set one of the most remarkable political survivals in the world. To the Manx it has always been a powerful and visible reminder that the Isle of Man is an ancient kingdom, enjoying its own Government, making its own laws, levying its own taxes and controlling its own expenditure. It is

Left: Tourism is still an important part of the economy. The sandy beaches provide a playground for children of all ages.

Photographed by Tony Lakin

Above: The gardens of Bishopscourt, Kirk Michael. Until the mid-seventies the ancient seat of the Bishop of Sodor and Mann.

Photographed by Alex Maddrell

also the scene of a ceremony which has survived a thousand years and whose disappearance would mark the end of the Manx as a nation.

Towards the end of July the annual Inter-Celtic Festival of Yn Chruinnaght is held at Ramsey. This week long festival of music, dance, art and literature of the six Celtic nations of Mann, Scotland, Ireland, Wales, Cornwall and Brittany is unique.

At the other end of the island another popular attraction is what is boastfully claimed as the World Tin Bath Championships, held in Castletown harbour. Competitors vie with each other to remain afloat whilst racing up the harbour in tin baths. The origins of this unusual event remain obscure!

In Peel, where most of the herrings are landed between June and September for smoking into the famous Manx kippers, Viking boat races involving teams each of ten people are held in August.

Towards the end of summer there is another sudden influx of the 'speed kings'. With a final burst of noise the Manx National Two-Day motorcycle trials, the Manx Grand Prix, the Manx International Car Rally and the Manx Classic Car races follow hot on each others' exhausts.

Almost as the last remaining visitors bid farewell to the island, proprietors of the small hotels and guest houses lock up their premises and, if the season has been rewarding, take off for their own holidays.

The island returns into the sole possession of those whose lives are bound up in its everyday life.

Top: Entering the water at Port Erin.
PHOTOGRAPHED BY JOHN NEIL

Above: The island hosts two international rallies every year.
PHOTOGRAPHED BY DAVID BOWERS

Left: 'Taking the bend' during International Cycle Week in July.
PHOTOGRAPHED BY MARTIN CASHEN

Right: Different styles of scramble racing on Peel beach!
PHOTOGRAPHED BY DAVID EVANS

Below: Yacht racing at Port St Mary.
PHOTOGRAPHED BY RICK TOMLINSON

Autumn

Heavy black tyre marks on many of the island's roads bear witness to the last of the summer road racing events. The days begin to shorten. Early morning mists and drenching dews presage the cooler weather to come. Smoke curls out of chimneys unused and dampened during the warmer months and the pleasant smell of burning vegetation give notice that gardeners are busy clearing for the winter.

Over the horizon the winds of the equinox are gathering their strength.

In the countryside, pigeons feed off the stubble of newly harvested corn and barley before yielding their places to the flocks of seagulls which follow the plough. Cock pheasants, having completed their moult, strut through the fields and along the roadsides. On the fells, the heather has quite lost the luminescent glow of mauve blossom it displayed in August; now it turns to brown and will soon revert to the black eclipse of winter.

Bilberries on the hillsides will already have been gathered but the hedgerows are now ready to be harvested by any who have the time and the inclination. Hips and blackberries grow in profusion and, in the early morning dews, some fields offer their mushroom crops to the early riser.

Almost before one realises it, the run-up to Christmas has started.

Winter proper has returned.

'I remember, I remember,

As the years go swiftly by,

That each season has its glory

Whether blue or grey the sky.

That the sadness of the autumn

And the beat of winter's rain

Are but stepping stones which bring us

To spring and summer once again.'

(*On a Manx Hillside* by Kathleen Faragher)

Previous Pages: Autumn colours at Injebreck Reservoir.
Photographed by Tony Lakin

Top Right: Turnstones race the surf at the Ayres beach.
Photographed by Jeremy Paul

Right: Sheep roam freely on the open hillsides.
Photographed by Michael Thompson - Eye of Man

Far Right: A stark reminder of the winter wind.
Photographed by Simon Park

PHOTOGRAPHED BY JEREMY PAUL

The Nature of Mann

By Michael Ingram

Some 10,000 years ago the Isle of Man was completely covered during the last Ice Age and cut off from mainland Great Britain. With the Irish Sea proving a formidable barrier to the spread of animals, today no large terrestrial mammals remain. The polecat ferret is the largest endemic mammal although foxes and hares have been re-introduced. For others the Irish Sea has proved too great a barrier. Squirrels, badgers and moles are conspicuous by their absence as are all forms of snake; although whether this is due to natural causes or to the intervention of St Patrick is a question for discussion.

Although the island lacks some of the more common species - Jays for example, others under pressure on the

Left: A dog leaps among a field of poppies near Castletown.
PHOTOGRAPHED BY ALEX MADDRELL

Top: Harvest Web
PHOTOGRAPHED BY MR. T. S. MARTIN

Right: Contrasting light in one of the island's many glens.
PHOTOGRAPHED BY MICHAEL THOMPSON - EYE OF MAN

mainland have found a safe haven. The breath-taking dive of a peregrine falcon as it hurtles out of the sky is no longer a rare sight. Neither is the roller-coaster trajectory of the hen harrier which competes with the falcon as a low level strike force.

Walk along the cliff tops overlooking the small islet known as the Calf of Man and the raucous cry of the Chough, 'the red-legged King of the Crows', rings loudly in your ears. A cool grey mist rolls inland across the Langness peninsula where *Stenobothus stigmaticus*, a rare grasshopper found nowhere else in the British Isles, clambers slowly between the long stems of grass. Waders feed noisily in the shallows along the shore. Teal, wigeon, flocks of mallard and many others sweep the pools with their bills. Overhead the air is loud with the indignant chatter of migrant chiff-chaff and willow warblers.

With the approach of spring the mood changes. Atlantic seals, which breed around the Calf of Man and at Maughold Head, spend their days basking on the rocks or diving beneath the gentle swell. The cliffs, so stark and inhospitable in winter, now become an ornithologists dream. Take a boat trip from Port Erin or Port St Mary and you can enjoy the view from a distance or land and become closer acquainted.

The cries of auks, kittiwakes and stiff winged fulmars echo between the sheer rock walls. Gannets dive into the open sea while Manx shearwaters (first described on the Isle of Man) skim elegantly across the wavetops. Shags and guillemots, oystercatchers and razorbills fill the air with colour and noise.

On the shingle beaches of the Point of Ayre at the northern tip of the island the terns - Arctic, common, little and Sandwich - skim acrobatically across the sea, their beaks heavy with a harvest of sand eels.

July brings dark shadows gliding majestically below the surface. The basking sharks have returned. Huge shapes (the largest can be up to 26 feet [8m] in length) move sedately through the water. It is a stately procession. At a mere three knots they travel across the ocean with sometimes as many as 50 in a shoal. Then, as suddenly as they appeared, their shadows blur until the last great fin dips below the surface. The Isle of Man is one of the few places in the world where these gentle

Below and right: Beautiful studies in nature.

Photographed by Simon Park

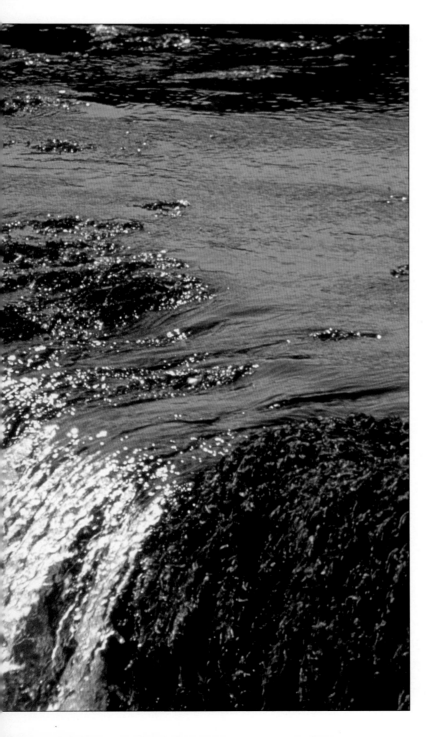

*Fuchsia grows wild in the mild climate
of the island.*
Top Left Photographed by Michael Thompson - Eye of Man
Top Right Photographed by Foley Vereker

*Bottom: "Maybe this wasn't such a good idea!" Swan and cygnets
about to go over the waterfall in Castletown harbour.*
Photographed by John Neil

monsters gather in any numbers. Little is known about their habits. They appear every year, sometimes three or four large shoals at a time and cruise around the island until September. There can be few sights more exhilarating than watching those black fins slicing through the water, the only sign of their passing the glitter of a phosphorescent wake in the moonlight.

Occasionally the taller, narrower fin of a killer whale, *Orcinus orca*, can seen further offshore but this is becoming increasingly rare.

The clear waters surrounding the island encourage a growing number of sport divers to spend their weekends exploring the world below the surface. For those not so tempted, hundreds of rock-pools teem with marine life around the shoreline; a fascinating way to spend a few hours with only the sound of the sea for company.

Inland, the purple and yellow of the gorse-fringed heather on the hillsides is interspersed with bluebells, as if an artist had spattered the canvas with blobs of paint. This is the territory of hawks and arctic hares, where the moorlands roll gently across the central spine of the island until the ground drops steeply into the dense tree-lined glens. Here beneath the overhanging branches where streams rush through glades of wild garlic common flowers such as dog's mercury and yellow archangel are absent, but spring squill is a pleasant surprise.

Whether in wooded glen or on windswept hillside the air is heavy with the tang of the sea.

A microcosm of the mainland the island has its own blend of wildlife. A valuable heritage to guard, cherish and share with others who can appreciate its uniqueness and beauty.

Top Far Left: The clear waters around the island are ideal for 'scuba' diving.
Bottom Far Left: A harmless basking shark cruises near the surface. As it moves through the sea large volumes of water enter its cavernous mouth and pass across its gills, where the plankton is sieved for food.
Left: Lobsters are no longer an easy catch.
Bottom Left: A velvet crab.
Below: The iridescent tentacles of the Lion's Mane jellyfish are designed to trap the unwary fish.
ALL PHOTGRAPHED BY DR BEN HEXTALL

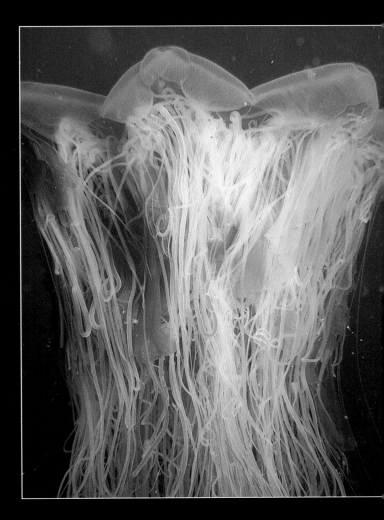

Left: A cuttlefish swims away from the camera.
Below left: Starfish feeding on the wide variety of encrusting animals that cover the sea bed near Port Erin.
Above: Conger Eel hiding among sea anemones and soft coral below the Burroo Rock beside the Calf of Man.

Above: A transparent 'comb jelly' swimming slowly through the clear water.
Below: Jewel anemones in the shallow water.
ALL PHOTGRAPHED BY DR BEN HEXTALL

Left: A statuesque heron waits patiently for an early morning meal.
PHOTGRAPHED BY JEREMY PAUL

Above: Razorbills.
PHOTGRAPHED BY SIMON PARK

Right: The ledges of the "Chasms" provide a crowded nesting area.
PHOTOGRAPHED BY RICK TOMLINSON

Below: Evening flight over Derbyhaven Bay.
PHOTOGRAPHED BY FOLEY VEREKER

Left: Late arrival.
PHOTOGRAPHED BY FOLEY VEREKER

Next Pages: An Atlantic Grey Seal sunbathes on a rock on the Calf of Man.
PHOTOGRAPHED BY RICK TOMLINSON

*Top far left and bottom far left:
Domestic animals are a natural part of
the island's scenery.*

PHOTOGRAPHED BY RICK TOMLINSON

Left: Cregneish farmyard.

PHOTOGRAPHED BY ALEX MADDRELL

*Below: The four-horned Loghtan sheep are
unique to the island.*

PHOTOGRAPHED BY ALEX MADDRELL

PHOTOGRAPHED BY MICHAEL THOMPSON

ISLAND OF CONTRASTS

BY MICHAEL INGRAM

All islands, by definition, can be considered to be 'offshore' but, in today's terminology, the title has become synonymous with self governing dependent territories. While the Isle of Man owes allegiance to the English Crown it is not part of the United Kingdom.

The island's position in the middle of the Irish Sea meant that, in the 18th century it was ideally placed as the centre for the smuggling trade. It requires little imagination to picture a column of shadowy figures, laden with contraband, snaking up the narrow hill path from a secluded bay. Even today the footpath from Fleshwick Bay crosses an area of land known as the 'Free States'... believed to be a reference to the avoidance of duty payable on certain goods that passed that way!

The purchase of the island in 1765 by the British Government (to stamp out the illegal trading) did not however, compromise the independence of the internal government. Today, Tynwald still promulgates its own laws as it has done for over a thousand years particularly with regard to taxation. Only in external matters does it defer to the United Kingdom. More recently the island has negotiated a special relationship with the European Community which allows free movement of goods between the two.

The curves and columns of the Legislative Buildings contrast with the straight lines of modern architecture.

PHOTOGRAPHED BY CREATIVE STUDIO

With such a well-established parliamentary system and long experience of managing its own affairs, the island brings a stability and long-term security to its independent 'offshore' status.

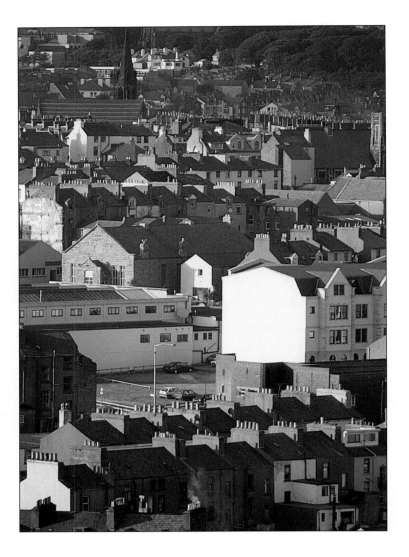

Over the centuries the island's fortunes have fluctuated but, since the mid 1970's the business and financial sector has grown in both confidence and stature. With the rapid growth of the Isle of Man as an international offshore financial centre came the need to strengthen the island's image and reputation.

Financial activities are properly supervised and effectively regulated by the Financial Supervision Commission (FSC) established by Tynwald in 1983. The FSC is charged with developing and operating systems to protect the interests of depositors and investors and the good name of the Isle of Man. It licenses and supervises all banks, investment businesses, collective investment schemes and building societies. Insurance companies are subject to strict actuarial supervision and here the Insurance Authority is the relevant supervisory body, with protection for life policy-holders provided by the Isle of Man's Statutory Protection Scheme. All stockbroking companies are Members of the International Stock Exchange and have access to the London market via the Automated Quotations System.

Change does not come easily to the people of the island. And why should it? There has always been 'Traa dy Liooar'... (time enough)! Such an attitude can be frustrating but, where the security of funds is concerned it perhaps helps to minimise the dangers inherent in today's fast moving world of commerce.

But how has this recent growth affected the infrastructure of an island that has moved at its own gentle pace for so many centuries? An island whose economy until the late 1900's depended almost exclusively on catches of herring and the success of the potato crop? Even the heyday of the tourist trade has faded as package holidays offered guaranteed sunshine in more exotic climes.

Today, 34% of the total income comes from the finance sector, with high technology manufacturing accounting for 11% and tourism now in third place with only 7%.

With time comes change.

The contryside and its pleasures exists in close harmony
with urban development.

ABOVE :PHOTOGRAPHED BY MICHAEL THOMPSON - EYE OF MAN

LEFT: PHOTOGRAPHED BY RICK TOMLINSON

To adapt needs vision and as the saying goes 'where there is no vision....the people perish'. The Isle of Man will not perish because it has the unique ability to absorb change. Admittedly not always quietly, often with much wailing and gnashing of teeth but, given 'time enough' it does adapt. Therein lies its strength.

Financial stability and growth depend upon a solid base that can be measured over the years. The island has this and more and with over 220 square miles of beautiful countryside, it has the room to expand to accommodate its growing population.

And it has other attractions. It is close to the UK (only 50 minutes flying time from London) with connections by both air and sea to many major cities. The international businessman can be home from his meeting long before his colleagues have battled their way clear of London's commuters. Even if your

workplace is a frantic hive of activity – as communications on the island are as advanced as in any office in London or New York – within minutes of leaving one slips quickly into the more leisurely pace of island life.

This is the strength of Mann; the old rubbing shoulders with the new – each giving to the other.

In Douglas, banks of the world are sandwiched between long established firms of lawyers, international insurance companies, building societies, unit trust, asset management and protection companies, corporate management, shipping and personnel companies. The modern merging with the longer standing traditional Manx businesses in the busy town centre.

The island uses sterling as its currency (albeit with Manx coinage and notes) but deposits are accepted in all major

The structures of industry impose their own kind of beauty onto a predominantly pastural landscape.

PHOTOGRAPHED BY MICHAEL INGRAM

TOP LEFT: PHOTOGRAPHED BY MICHAEL THOMPSON - EYE OF MAN

BOTTOM LEFT: PHOTOGRAPHED BY SUE SNOW

currencies of the world. Operating within a statutory frame-work laid down under the Banking Act, banks offer a full range of services.

New buildings balance the old as the demand for office space continues. Hotels, once tied to the days of the 'summer visitor' of the past, adapt urgently to new demands for 'short break' holidays or business trips – and the needs of the environmentally conscious visitors intent on enjoying the wealth of natural beauty that the island has to offer.

The island is English speaking although Manx Gaelic is undergoing a resurgence. It is also a haven of peace and safety in a world where such values are becoming increasingly more difficult to find.

Long before the bustle of modern business starts the telephone lines humming and the computer discs whirring, the fishing boats have slipped quietly out of the harbours – as they have done for centuries past. There are fewer now and with catch quotas decreasing and fishing stocks disappearing, the industry is a shadow of its former self. Gone are the days when the jetties were tiered twelve feet (3.7m) high with herring barrels ready to salt down the catch. Smoke still hangs low over Peel as the smokeries 'cure' the catch and Manx kippers are still a much sought after delicacy, but the days when the 'drifters' filled the harbours from one side to the other have passed quietly into the mists of

time. Now the local boats spend their time searching for delicacies to grace the tables of the restaurants of Europe. Early morning in the cargo centre at Ronaldsway airport and boxes of scallops (and the smaller Queen scallop) are stacked beside fresh cut roses, aeroplane machine parts, kettle elements, live trout eggs and a variety of other specialised high value products. Until recently the air would have been loud with the scratching of crated lobsters bound for the huge 'vivaria' tanks in Antwerp and Paris but, again that is a sound of the past. Today the inshore fisherman is more likely to set his pots early in the morning and spend the rest of the day ferrying visitors to view sea birds and seals.

With the groundswell of interest in the environment and the conservation of nature, the island has a potential wealth

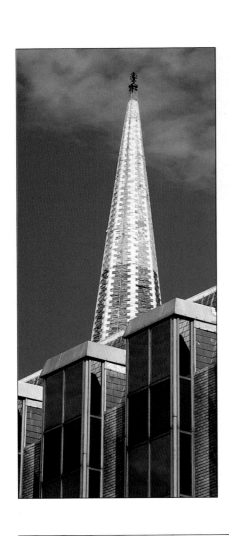

different to that created by the finance industry. It may not be as valuable in hard currency but if exploited with vision and understanding, who knows what the future may bring... in 'time enough'?

Although the Manx fishing fleet has declined over the years the 'Manx registered' fleet has grown dramatically as ship management companies have found the island to be a secure harbour for their business. International ship management, together with the associated companies, is one of the fastest growth areas in the island's economy.

With plans for marinas and an enthusiastic sailing, diving and watersport fraternity visible any weekend the sea allows, marine recreation is an expanding activity.

Above: The Jubilee Clock marks where the busy Victoria Street in Douglas meets the Promenade.
PHOTOGRAPHED BY CREATIVE STUDIO

Left: Victorian buildings designed to accomodate tourists during the 'boom era' of the late nineteenth century.

Far Left: Merging the old with the new, is where planners of today need a vision of tommorow.
PHOTOGRAPHED BY RICK TOMLINSON

Inland, farming is still an integral part of the infrastructure and over 75% of the land is in agricultural use. Cattle and sheep graze contentedly on the rich hillsides. On the Calf of Man and in several protected areas on the main island the native Manx breed of sheep, the Loghtan, is of interest to casual visitor and professional breeder alike. The breed is unusual in that it carries a light brown fleece and the rams can produce two or even three pairs of fearsome looking horns. A fact to be born in mind when taking a short cut across a field.

An ear flicks lazily as the early morning commuter jet lifts into the sky bound for London; a head turns in idle curiosity as a motorbike roars past on the other side of the hedge. Unique again is a legislature which allows public roads to be used as race tracks. The eternal quest for speed rubs shoulders with a countryside that has changed little over the centuries.

Right and Inset Right: "Over 75% of the land is in agricultural use."
PHOTOGRAPHED BY TONY LAKIN
PHOTOGRAPHED BY K. SMITH

Below: The control centre of the electricity generating station.
PHOTOGRAPHED BY MICHAEL THOMPSON - EYE OF MAN

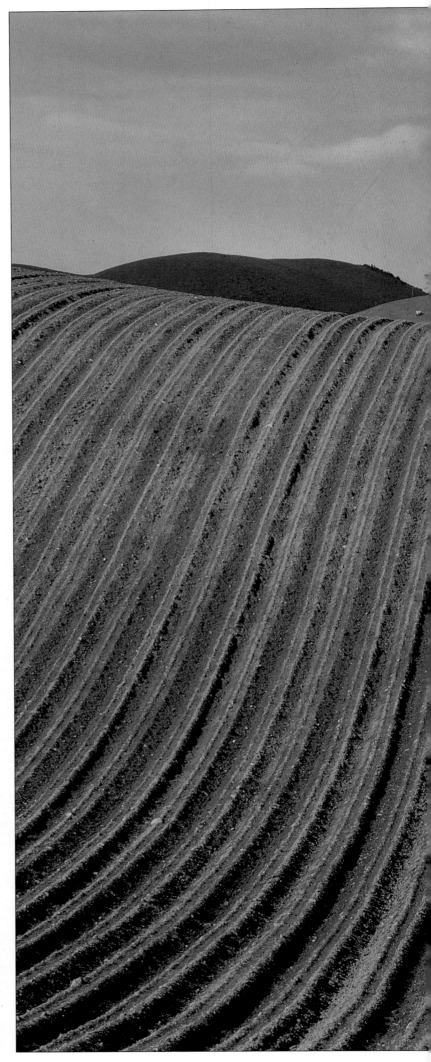

Each year in June the scent of the honeysuckle is smothered by that of hot metal and burning rubber...as motorcycles and their riders do wondrous things along Douglas promenade while the Red Arrows leave twisted 'contrails' in the sky.

It is TT fortnight; a time when the jet-setting businessman makes sure he has booked his tickets well in advance.

Throughout the year such sporting events can catch the unwary off guard. Classic car races and hill climbs create watery-eyed nostalgia as the bellow of a 'full-blown' Bentley deafens the ears. International rally cars hurtle along the narrow country lanes. In July grim-faced cyclists flash past in a blur of colour during International Cycling week. At sea the round-the-island RIB (Rigid Inflatable) boat races disturb the tranquillity for a couple of days in the year.

On the western shores the ancient ruins of Peel Castle peer down impassively. Those empty battlements have seen it all before. Modern day adventurers now launch their sleek craft across the same sandy beach where Vikings first landed a thousand years ago.

Inland the contrasts are the same. Prehistoric ramparts cast long shadows over the graves of early kings and princes. In the valleys, 'high tech' factories produce a wide variety of high quality equipment. Aircraft parts accurately machined to the most stringent specifications; specialised heating elements,

The Steam Packet ferry terminal, Douglas.

PHOTOGRAPHED BY RICK TOMLINSON

The sound of the whistle of the 'Groudle Glen' steam train lingers in a million memories.

PHOTOGRAPHED BY MIRIAM CRITCHLOW

optical laser equipment, 'state of the art' wallpaper printing machines, shoes and a wide spectrum of other high quality exports. As a base for manufacture the commercial viability of products is dictated by competitive shipping rates. The most successful products tend to be small, low weight, high precision and high value. The island also boasts Europe's first and, to date, only offshore freeport where goods can be shipped in and out without incurring taxes. Local industry is building on the long term stability of the business community and this is one of the greatest natural treasures that the Isle of Man has to offer – the ability to combine the old with the new – the fast with the slow – all on the canvas of a beautiful island framed by the clear waters of the Irish Sea.

Whether powering towards it in a space-age 'Sea Cat' or lifting into the skies above the mediaeval fortress of Castle Rushen, the island is linked to the world by the latest transport and telecommunications systems. But once out of the office it takes only a few minutes to reach the tranquil anonymity of the mountain paths or the seashore.

The success of the island in developing the business sector has brought with it pressures on land. Continuous stable growth is always difficult to achieve while at the same time retaining a viable infrastructure. Nowhere is this more clearly illustrated than in the sprawling mass of dormitory towns that surround the great cities of the world. It is here that the 'vision' of the planners has to be at its most perceptive. An island is a critically balanced ecosystem bounded by immovable borders. The Isle of Man leads the way in its diversity as an offshore centre and its people, by virtue of their long history, have developed a pragmatic outlook on life. Today a vibrant business heart beats strongly within a beautiful but delicate framework. Only the future will tell if this balance can be maintained.

For all the high finance it is perhaps well to remember that when Christmas Eve, perhaps the most lucrative trading day of the year, falls on half-day closing, the shutters may still come down at lunchtime!

Traa dy Liooar! There is always... 'time enough'.

Fast or slow? The island accomodates all tastes.

PHOTOGRAPHED BY RICK TOMLINSON

Above: The new Seacat started operations to the mainland in 1994.
PHOTOGRAPHED BY ISLAND PHOTOGRAPHICS

Left: The refurbished Groudle Glen railway trundles along the coast
at a more leisurely pace.
PHOTOGRAPHED BY FOLEY VEREKER

Below: The "VSV" at speed. A revolutionary new craft,
designed and built on the island.
PHOTOGRAPHED BY RICK TOMLINSON

*Sometimes the island echoes to the roar of TT exhausts, at others it
sleeps peacefully beneath 'Manannan's cloak'.*

ABOVE: PHOTOGRAPHED BY DOUG BAIRD

RIGHT: PHOTOGRAPHED BY EDGAR BOYES

Milner's Tower casts a long shadow over Bradda Head.

PHOTOGRAPHED BY SIMON COX

Status Quo *in concert during TT Fortnight.*

PHOTOGRAPHED BY TONY LAKIN

'... and always there is the sea.'

PHOTOGRAPHED BY ROSEMARY GREENWOOD

PHOTOGRAPHED BY JEREMY PAUL

EVENING REFLECTIONS

The island experiences some of the most spectacular sunsets
in the world. The following pages recall a few of them.

PHOTOGRAPHED BY CREATIVE STUDIO

LEFT: PHOTOGRAPHED BY DR. BEN HEXTALL

TOP: PHOTOGRAPHED BY MARTIN CASHEN

ABOVE: PHOTOGRAPHED BY CREATIVE STUDIO

PHOTOGRAPHED BY MARTIN CASHEN

PHOTOGRAPHED BY RICK TOMLINSON

An Extract from Manx National Anthem

WORDS BY W.H. GILL. MANX TRANSLATION BY J.J. KNEEN.

O Land of our birth

O gem of God's earth

O island so strong and so fair

Built firm as Barrule

Thy throne of Home Rule

Make us free as thy sweet mountain air

O Halloo nyn ghooie

O 'Chliegeen ny s 'bwaaie

Ry ghedyn er ooir aalin Yee

Ta dt' Ardstoyl Reill-Thie

Myr Baarool er ny hoie

Dy reayll shin ayns seyrsnys as shee.

"Bradda Head from Poyll Vaaish"

PHOTOGRAPHED BY JOHN ATKINSON.

WINNER OF THE MOODS OF MANN PHOTOGRAPHIC COMPETITION.

SPONSORS

The Editors wish to convey their thanks for the support and encouragement given
by the following companies who made the production possible.

AIB Bank (Isle of Man) Limited

Alexander Insurance Managers (Isle of Man) Limited

Bank of Bermuda (Isle of Man) Limited

Barclays Bank Plc & Barclays Finance Co. (IOM) Ltd

Bibby International Services (IOM) Limited

Bradford & Bingley (Isle of Man) Limited

Dorchester Maritime Limited

Island Express Limited

Isle of Man Assurance Limited

Isle of Man Newspapers Limited

The Isle of Man Steam Packet Co. Ltd

KWB Kenmac Limited

Lloyds Bank Plc

Manx Airlines Limited

Manx Telecom Limited

MeesPierson (Isle of Man) Limited

Midocean Maritime Limited

Mount Murray Country Club

Northwest Trust Limited

The Royal Bank of Scotland (IOM) Limited

Scottish Provident International

Sefton Hotel Plc

Sun Life International

Warburg Asset Management Isle of Man Ltd

'Moods of Mann.'

ABOVE: PHOTOGRAPHED BY MICHAEL THOMPSON - EYE OF MAN

LEFT: PHOTOGRAPHED BY ROSEMARY GREENWOOD